BMW M-SERIES

BMW M-SERIES

The Complete Story

Alan Henry

First Published in 1992 by
The Crowood Press Ltd
Ramsbury, Marlborough
Wiltshire SN8 2HR

Paperback edition 1998

British Library Cataloguing in Publication Data

A catalogue record for this book is available from the British
Library.

ISBN 1 86126 146 2

Picture Credits
The majority of the photographs in this book were supplied by the
Motoring Picture Library, Beaulieu. Additional photographs were
supplied by BMW and the author.

Acknowledgements

The author would like to acknowledge the wide-ranging assistance
he has received from Chris Willows, Public Affairs Manager of
BMW (GB), his colleague Friedbert Holz from the Munich
company's press office and BMW Motorsport GmbH Managing
Director Karl-Heinz Kalbfell. Thanks are also due to Bob Murray,
Michael Harvey and Shaun Campbell of *Autocar & Motor*
magazine for permission to quote from their road-test material; to
Classic and Sports Car magazine for permission to quote from
Chris Willows' article on Alex von Falkenhausen; to David
Tremayne of *Motoring News* for permission to reproduce the track
test that the author carried out on the BMW M1 Procar in 1979.

Typeset by Chippendale Type Ltd., Otley, West Yorkshire.
Printed and bound by Times Offset, Malaysia

Contents

M-Series Key Dates

1972 : BMW Motorsport GmbH established as a separate company operating out of premises at Preussenstrasse, Munich. Main priority from the start was operation and maintenance of BMW's racing programme.

1978 : BMW M1 unveiled as high performance central-engined road machine intended to race in Group 5 sports car events. Fitted with 3.5-litre 24-valve six-cylinder engine it was used in exclusive Procar series and later became collector's piece with only 454 manufactured.

1980 : Manufacture of the first M535i high performance road car carrying BMW identification. Equipped with stiffened suspension and distinctive external visual identification, it represented the first application of BMW competition experience in a production-derived road car.

1984 : BMW M635CSi introduced to enhance 6-series saloon range. During its five year run just under 6,000 of these cars would be produced, powered by the same 24-valve 3.5-litre six-cylinder engine as used in the M1. First M5 saloon, based on the second generation 5-series bodyshell, to be built exclusively by BMW Motorsport introduced.

1985 : M535i introduced to supplement the range, although this in effect was only a badged 535i.

1986 : BMW M3 saloon introduced, initially with a 2.3-litre four-cylinder engine which would eventually grow to 2.5-litres by 1990. Homologation for competition application was foremost in BMW's mind when producing this car, but it was to prove commercially the most successful M-car with a production run in excess of 14,000.

1988 : New M5 introduced based on slightly larger, lighter third generation 5-series bodyshell. Built at new BMW Motorsport manufacturing facility at Garching, near Munich. M3 convertible also introduced this year.

Introduction

BMW'S MOTORSPORT HERITAGE

The distinctive blue and white propellor motif of the Bayerische Motoren Werke is synonymous with motoring exclusivity and high performance. The Munich-based company today occupies a position of prestige and respect on the international motoring scene which reflects discriminatingly Germanic standards of engineering and attention to detail. These have earned it a position alongside Porsche and Mercedes-Benz as one of the world's great marques.

Moreover, like Porsche and Mercedes-Benz, it has always fostered a deep-rooted commitment to motorsport. For BMW, motorsport has become a way of life and an attitude of mind. The company does not go motor racing simply for promotional purposes, although in the harsh economic environment of the 1990s, this is clearly a major factor. It goes motor racing because it believes that it can make a better product for the everyday customer if its technicians and engineers have been subjected to the intensity of competition, the uncompromising deadlines and the demands for engineering perfection which are necessarily generated by such an involvement.

A new motorsports era began for the company when it took the decision, in 1980, to begin supplying its turbocharged Formula 1 engines to the Brabham Grand Prix team. This triggered a decision to use the letter 'M' to formalize a trend which had started three years earlier with the development of the M1 coupe. It was intended to symbolize the motorsporting heritage of the company's high performance products.

Soon this nomenclature would be used as a running theme linking together a variety of apparently very different products – from Grand Prix engines (MPower) to a collection of sportswear fashions (MStyle), from highly sophisticated technical equipment (MTechnics) to the motorsport team itself, operating in a variety of categories (MTeam).

BMW was anxious to propel this image forward into its marketing strategy during the early 1980s, in an attempt to unite a special range of products under a single banner, thereby underlining the company's commitment to motorsport as a whole.

The ultimate embodiment of this commitment can be seen in the current range of M-series BMWs. Exclusive, beautifully built motor cars with titanic performance, yet imbued with flexibility, docility and huge margins of operational safety. Yet the M-series cars represent merely the latest confection in a long line of competition-bred machines which have all done their fair share to embellish and enhance the status of BMW since their first competition successes were achieved almost sixty years ago.

Well before the adoption of this formal method of identification, BMW were making cars that were always slightly out of the ordinary. The company's historical roots were buried firmly in Germany's fledgeling aviation industry. But although it began motorcycle manufacture in 1922, another six years would pass before BMW absorbed the Eisenach-based Dixi company and became involved in the car-making business.

From 1929, the company's fortunes for the next twenty turbulent years were largely steered by Franz-Josef Popp – his daughter Erica would marry Mercedes-Benz Grand

Prix star Dick Seaman in 1938 – during which the company was steadily built up and then virtually smashed to pieces by the devastation of the Second World War.

HUMBLE BEGINNINGS

The first BMW cars were Austin Sevens built under licence, the legacy of a deal forged by Dixi. From July 1929, these Dixi-Sevens began to benefit from a gradual refining process with more local content being incorporated and the addition of such refinements as four-wheel braking.

BMW's increasing confidence and sense of enterprise encouraged it to expand its technical horizons, cancelling the Austin Seven licensing agreement on 1 March 1932 to concentrate on the manufacture of its own 3/20 saloon which featured swing-axle suspension all round.

From the outset, BMW projected an imaginative, thrusting image and the 3/20 was followed up in June 1933 by the 1.2-litre six-cylinder 303. The first batch of steel-pressed bodies for the 303 was ironically produced by the Daimler Benz company at Sindelfingen, a firm destined to become one of BMW's greatest rivals in the post-war era.

The 303 model quickly earned a reputation as a good-handling car, further enhancing BMW's image. It was eventually discontinued in 1934 to be replaced by the 900cc, four-cylinder 309 and the 1.5-litre, six-cylinder 315 – the latter establishing the company's aspirations towards making high-performance racing machinery.

Opposite *The ultimate embodiment of the M-series philosophy is summed up by the latest M5 saloon, the most discreet and unobtrusive 'Q car' imaginable.*

RISE AND FALL

The evolution of the German *autobahns* of the 1930s as part of Hitler's strategy for facilitating troop movements had a strong secondary effect amongst the car-buying public. Demand increased for machines capable of sustained high-speed cruising, producing those speeds without mechanical trouble and offering a high standard of all-round roadworthiness.

Typical of the sort of high performance offered during that period was the rakish BMW 315/1 sport cabriolet which was manufactured between 1934 and 1936. With three Solex carburettors and a high compression ratio, BMW guaranteed to its purchasers that it would reach 75mph (120kph). This was followed by the same triple carburettor set-up applied to the 1,911cc engine in the 319/1, all this development reaching its apotheosis in the 328, the car which did more for BMW's pre-war image than possibly any other machine.

Bearing in mind that only 462 such machines were manufactured, the 328 could be said to have had an effect on the company's development totally disproportionate to its financial contribution to the balance sheet. Yet as a fast tourer, a road racer and an inspiration to both Jaguar and Bristol in their post-war endeavours, the BMW 328 earned itself a unique niche in the German company's history.

Then came the dark days of war. Germany was utterly devastated and, by the time hostilities ended in 1945, was divided down the middle as the Iron Curtain slammed down between the Baltic and the Adriatic. Eisenach was now trapped in the Communist bloc and the factories in Munich looked set to be razed by order of the American Military Government.

Mercifully, the latter order was countermanded. The company then scraped a living, literally from the gutter, manufacturing bicycles, pots and pans, garden equipment, or anything else that came its way. The frustrations of those immediate post-war years were compounded when the old Eisenach factory, under Russian control, began producing low-quality facsimilies under the BMW badge. But a successful legal action saw them off and the East German machines had to be renamed EMWs as a result.

THE BRITISH CONNECTION

The Aldington family, who owned the Frazer Nash (AFN) company in England, had left a BMW 328 in Germany for the duration of hostilities, and H. J. Aldington managed to make a visit to Munich shortly after the end of the war. He returned with one of the special 328s which had been built for the shortened 1940 Mille Miglia event, rather than his own machine.

AFN became involved with the Bristol company in the immediate aftermath of the war. The aircraft company had decided on a move into the car production business in order to hedge its bets in the event of aircraft production taking a peacetime downturn. H.J. Aldington showed Bristol his BMW 327 which proved the inspiration for the first post-war Bristol 200 and, as they appeared to be travelling along the same route, it was agreed that Bristol would acquire a majority stake in AFN.

To assist the Bristol project, H.J. and Don Aldington acquired all the technical plans and details of the 326, 327 and 328 BMWs, plus some other associated prototype material, under the guise of war reparation. Bristol began making its own version of the 328 engine for eventual use in the 400 coupe, and the alliance with AFN was formally dissolved in 1947. Frazer Nash began manufacturing its own machines, still benefiting from a cordial relationship with Bristol, who willingly continued to supply them with the four-cylinder engines.

BACK FROM THE ASHES

By 1949, the BMW company had sparked into life again, taking the audacious decision that what was needed to re-establish the company's reputation was a large luxury saloon. It was one hell of a gamble under the circumstances, because Germany's economy remained in a parlous position for much of the early 1950s. In addition, just as BMW's flame flickered tentatively, the whole of Europe was adversely affected by the 1955 Suez crisis, the long-term effects of which would bring BMW back to the brink of financial disaster towards the end of that same decade.

Yet the decision was taken. The first serious post-war BMW would be the 501 saloon – initially manufactured with a 2-litre, 65bhp six-cylinder engine – which was first displayed at the 1951 Frankfurt Motor Show but which took another eighteen months to get into production.

Production facilities were enhanced in 1953 when the company managed to purchase its own body press facilities, thanks to finance made available under the Marshall Aid programme. Gone was the need to rely on the slow, bespoke manufacturing process of the Stuttgart-based Bauer coachbuilding company which produced the initial run of 501s.

Perhaps predictably, the market that had been so optimistically anticipated just wasn't there and BMW had to do some urgent and strategic tinkering with both price structure and specification. A 72bhp engine was introduced in March 1954, the price slashed by almost ten per cent, and a lower specification 501B model introduced to widen the customer catchment area.

The Geneva Motor Show in March 1954 saw the arrival of the 2.6-litre V8-engined version. This low-revving push-rod unit, which developed 100bhp with an impressive smoothness, was widely acclaimed as one of the most refined power units of its era.

Symbolic of the progress achieved by BMW across half a century of car making, the 1929 3/15 Dixi poses with the 1979 M1 sports coupe, the first of the M-series machines which did so much to raise the German company's competition orientated profile.

But the BMW 501 V8 was desperately expensive. As Eric Dymock points out in his excellent *BMW – A Celebration*, the 502 was priced in England at a daunting £2,459, inclusive of tax and import duties – and this was at a time when a Riley Pathfinder cost £1,411 and even a Jaguar XK140 only £1,693.

Dubbed the 'Baroque Angels' because of their extrovert, flowing lines, the 501/502 nevertheless endured a production run of almost a decade, surviving through to 1961 as the 120mph (190kph) 3200S, before finally being withdrawn from the market.

SPORTING FIT

During the 1950s, BMW was absent from the motorsport arena, but still pursued its commitment to the sporting ethic. During those financially straitened times, undoubtedly one of the company's most striking products was the 507 coupe and convertible. It was styled by Count Albrecht Goetz, whose subsequent design work on the Datsun 240Z would prove a tremendous success in the early 1970s.

When one looks at the 507's specifications in retrospect, one might be forgiven for

In 1972, BMW unveiled a dramatic sports coupe; but the M1 was not announced for sale until 1978.

The Munich company started producing this tiny three-wheeler, with its front-opening door, under a licensing agreement in 1955. Over 161,000 Isettas were sold between 1955 and 1962, after which point the onset of the swinging sixties and the return of cheap petroleum quickly caused it to go out of fashion.

From a statistical viewpoint, the Isetta was the best-selling BMW to date, but the profit margin on each unit was perilously small. The 'stretched' four-seater Isetta led through logically to the development of the rear-engined Michelotti-styled BMW 700. The latter was the company's first foray into small car manufacturing and sold 190,000 units between 1959 and 1965.

(Opposite) *The BMW 507 kept the Munich company's sporting image to the forefront of quality motoring in the mid-1950s.*

Nevertheless, by the end of the 1950s BMW was losing money at an alarming rate, a process which had been aggravated by an unsuccessful return to the aero-engine business. Pressure from the banks for a merger with Mercedes-Benz was successfully resisted by loyal shareholders, who stood firm against a backdrop of changing management which did not really stabilize until 1959.

Not until the early years of the 1960s did BMW finally turn this difficult corner. Sustained financial success provided the base for the manufacture of a range of cars. Notable milestones amongst these included the square-cut BMW 1500 saloon of 1962–64 and the sensational 2002ti of 1968. The 2002ti would not only begin paving the way for today's highly regarded cars from Munich, but also give the company the hardware with which to open its sustained motorsport challenge of the post-war generation.

1 Where the Motorsport Began

Back in the 1930s Mercedes-Benz and Auto Union ruled the international Grand Prix stage. But BMW didn't lag behind in the race to uphold the international sporting achievements of the Fatherland. In this connection, the most significant date must be regarded as 14 June 1936, when Ernst Henne gave the 328 its race debut in the Eifelrennen at the Nürburgring, coming away with victory in the up-to-2-litre class.

BMW was encouraged by the Nazis to contest sports car races on an international basis: Le Mans, the Mille Miglia and the Tourist Trophy. The 1938 Mille Miglia saw a 2-litre class victory for the 328 driven by the dashing young Englishman A.F.P. Fane, later killed on active service with the RAF, while these cars finished took fifth, seventh and ninth places in the last Le Mans 24-hour race prior to the war the following summer.

BMW's competition lineage took off seriously for the first time with the type 328 in the immediate pre-war years. In this special 2-litre sports car race held prior to the 1938 German Grand Prix, virtually the entire field is made up of 328s, the winner being Paul Greifzu in car number 10.

Two of the 328s take the deeply banked Karussell corner at the Nürburgring during the same race.

Racing continued in Italy through to 1940 when the Mille Miglia was held on a truncated 104-mile (63km) route over a triangular circuit between Brescia–Cremona–Mantua–Brescia. This event was won by Huschke von Hanstein and Walter Baumer. Von Hanstein, of course, would later do more than his fair share for Germany's post-war motor racing renaissance, first as Porsche's highly respected Competitions Manager and later as a delegate to the FIA.

Racing and sports car development continued at BMW as unobtrusively as possible through 1940 with preparations for a 2.5-litre, 150bhp twin overhead camshaft version of the 328 planned for the 1941 Mille Miglia. In the event, the race was understandably overwhelmed by other considerations and never took place.

RACING EXPLOITS

Any account of BMW's post-war competition achievements inevitably must have Alex von Falkenhausen as one of its central characters. A BMW motorcycle engineer in the 1930s, von Falkenhausen had his own 328 which emerged from hiding to contest the first post-war motor sporting event to be held in Germany. (This was a hillclimb at Ruehstein in the Black Forest, held during July 1946.) Von Falkenhausen finished second behind Hermann Lang, the 1939 European Champion, who was driving the 1940 Mille Miglia winning coupe.

Suitably encouraged, and with several 328 engines at his disposal, von Falkenhausen built his own racing special which he christened the ALFA-BMW. His interpretation of the famous Italian acronym came

Alex von Falkenhausen

Freiherr Alex von Falkenhausen was born in the artistic Schwabing district of Munich in 1907. From an early age, he developed an interest in mechanical matters. He went on to study successfully for an engineering degree, after which he became passionately involved in motorcycle racing.

Whilst racing a British Calthorpe in 1932, he was noticed by the fledgeling BMW company. They offered him a job as a chassis engineer, and he continued to work on motorcycle projects up until the start of the Second World War. He also developed a passionate interest in cars during the thirties.

Von Falkenhausen successfully acquired a BMW-built Dixi 3/15, a BMW 315/1 and, in 1939, a 328 – which was fortunate to escape the effect of the hostilities.

With an enormous sense of enthusiasm and enterprise, von Falkenhausen struck out on his own in the immediate post-war years, manufacturing a series of racing specials under the AFM banner, which relied on highly modified BMW engines for their motive power. Several such machines were built, but financing the operation proved a highly precarious business. The programme trickled to a halt in the early 1950s.

In 1954, when Fritz Fiedler returned from his 'secondment' to Fraser Nash in England, von Falkenhausen was invited to return to BMW to run the racing department. Initially, he was to concentrate solely on motorcycle competition.

Together with former Auto Union star Hans Stuck, von Falkenhausen used a competition version of the 507 sports car in some minor events, but couldn't seriously challenge the Maseratis, Porsches and Ferraris which were conceived from the ground up as competition cars.

Still, von Falkenhausen used his venerable BMW 328 in the early 1950s, winning the 1951 and 1953 Austrian Alpine Rallies and the 1952 French Alpine. Then the car was retired and, from there on, he would concentrate on using a variety of off-the-peg machines, including the 502 saloon and the tiny 700 coupe well into the mid-1960s, having risen to the status of BMW's Chief Engineer in 1957.

The 700 made its race debut in March 1960 and enabled Hans Stuck Snr to round off his professional driving career on a high note by using the little coupe to win the touring car class of the German Hillclimb Championship. He proved extremely adept at getting his own way within the company by stealth and subtle persuasion and was always regarded as a very popular personality.

In 1961 von Falkenhausen enjoyed no fewer than ten competition outings in the BMW 700, emerging with class victories on every occasion. Increasingly, the little rear-engined cars would make international racing forays outside Germany and became quite a force to be reckoned with in the smallest capacity of the European Touring Car Championship.

Von Falkenhausen's final competitive outing came at Hockenheim in September 1965 when he drove the ex-Dan Gurney works Brabham Formula 1 car, fitted with the experimental Apfelbeck radial-valve 2-litre BMW engine. With this machine he launched a successful onslaught on the half-mile and 500 metres World records, presaging the official Brabham-BMW Grand Prix alliance by some sixteen years!

In 1972 the arrival of Jochen Neerpasch as Competitions manager led to the establishment of BMW Motorsport as a separate company, but von Falkenhausen continued in charge of design until his retirement from the company in 1975 at the age of sixty-eight. In his final years with the company he remained supportive and enthusiastic about the Competition programme and offered Neerpasch as much behind-the-scenes support as he could muster, in no way feeling that the younger man had undermined his status within the company.

Alex von Falkenhausen died in 1989, at the grand old age of eighty-two years, having contributed more than any other single individual to the sporting image of the company to which he devoted his life.

The CSL's straight-six engine produced 430bhp at 8,500rpm at the height of its works-backed development.

He came too late to salvage any realistic semblance of a works-supported effort and, indeed, factory support was limited to financial bonuses paid out to the best-placed private runners of the impressive-looking 3-litre engined BMW 2800CS coupes. There were also plans for the famous Broadspeed tuning establishment to run a BMW CS in the British Championship for John Fitzpatrick. But behind-the-scenes politicking ensured that this project never got off the ground.

The 1972 European Touring Car Championship was fought out in three capacity classes across nine events. Ford's Cologne competitions department, now under the stewardship of Mike Kranefuss (today the Detroit-based boss of Ford's worldwide racing efforts), fielded a squad of 2.9-litre Capri RS saloons which steamrollered their way to seven victories.

(Overleaf) *Joachim Winkelhock's Schnitzer team M3 leads a trio of Mercedes 190E 2.5-16s through the stadium at Hockenheim, during one of the two rounds of the 1991 German Touring Car Championship to be held at the circuit near Heidelberg.*

Altfrid Heger's Linder Team M3 in the pits at Zolder – the Belgian circuit which hosted the first round of the 1991 German Touring Car Championship.

Jarier at the wheel, the works March-BMW raced to eight wins out of nineteen starts to clinch the European Formula 2 Championship for the Anglo-German alliance in their first year together.

Throughout the 1970s, the story of Formula 2 was the story of March-BMW domination, with Patrick Depailler's works March-BMW winning the European Championship in 1974, Schnitzer also supplemented the efforts of BMW Motorsport by producing his own

engine, which propelled Jacques Laffite's Elf-backed Martini to the title in 1975. There was a strength in depth to BMW's Formula 2 involvement which was to prove remarkably long-lasting.

A slight hiccup occurred in 1976 and 1977 when Jean-Pierre Jabouille and René Arnoux, using Renault V6 power, won the European title. But both March and BMW pushed themselves to the hilt in 1978 and Bruno Giacomelli emerged with the

One of the Group 5 racing 320s being prepared for the Junior Team in the race shop at BMW Motorsport GmbH, early 1977.

Championship laurels. The blue and white colour co-ordinated BMW house livery was again projected strongly throughout that season – Giacomelli and team-mates Surer and Winkelhock running under the 'BMW Junior Team F2' identification.

In 1979, Marc Surer retained the Championship for March-BMW. The following year, however, the production-based BMW four was roundly defeated by the all-aluminium Brian Hart 420R engine installed in the works Toleman TG280 driven by Brian Henton. In 1981 the challenge of the new Honda V6 propelled Geoff Lees's works Ralt to the European

Championship. Although Corrado Fabi would take the final March-BMW Formula 2 title the following year, the momentum of the Japanese company's burgeoning involvement proved too strong. Honda won the last two European Championship titles before Formula 2 gave way to Formula 3000 at the start of 1985.

By then, of course, BMW Motorsport GmbH would be deeply involved in Formula 1 as engine supplier to the Brabham team and Neerpasch would be gone from the company head office in Preussenstrasse. His departure from the company in 1979 is

TO THE PRESENT

In 1986, BMW Motorsport GmbH expanded its factory capacity with the opening of a new plant at Garching, east of Munich. This is where the M5s – and later the M3 convertibles – were manufactured in high-tech surroundings of immaculate, clinical cleanliness. Whilst the M5s were treated as hand-made specialist automobiles, the M3 and M635CSi road cars were always manufactured on BMW's main production line.

In 1990, Karlheinz Kalbfell took over the post of BMW Motorsport GmbH Managing Director, at a time when the company's racing commitment was focussed solely on the prestigious German Touring Car Championship. Kalbfell feels strongly that the rival Audi team only won the title in 1990 'because the authorities failed to impose a handicap on their Quattro saloons. In 1991 we plan to strike back with an even more powerful 350bhp engine and, for 1992, we will be preparing a further revised car which should deliver close to 400bhp.'

Kalbfell's ambitions were to be thwarted in 1991 as Mercedes took the title again, but it remains to be seen what BMW Motorsport can produce in the future. The third generation 3-series, forming the basis for a new M3 racer from the start of 1992, will prove the decisive factor.

All the racing M3s were obviously built by the Motorsport division and, by the middle of 1991, they had sold more than 250 kits at about £90,000 apiece, a price which did not include assembly or any maintenance work.

The majority of the 480 Motorsport employees concentrate their efforts on road cars such as the M3 and M5. Up to 1991 the M3 was easily the best-selling M model, but demand dropped off considerably when the wraps came off the latest 3-series range.

'In 1990 we manufactured somewhere in the region of 3,000 M3s,' explained Kalbfell, 'but business slowed down considerably in 1991, although we expect it to pick up

Wolfgang Peter Flohr was in charge of BMW Motorsport GmbH from 1985 to 1988 before leaving to join the ADAC and then Lancia Deutschland.

detailed within the section covering BMW's Formula 1 involvement (*see* p177).

His place was taken by former journalist Dieter Stappert, previously Neerpasch's number two. It was Stappert who presided over the politically delicate Formula 1 years, working with the Brabham Grand Prix Team and its chief Bernie Ecclestone. Stappert was succeeded in 1985 by Wolfgang Peter Flohr, whose commercial management expertise was responsible for initiating an ambitious expansion programme. By 1985, BMW Motorsport had expanded its turnover to around 70 million Deutschmarks, somewhere in the region of £24 million at the contemporary exchange rate.

dramatically when we start a big push with the new-bodied M3, which owes a lot to the M5.' The big M5 saloon is currently rated as the Motorsport division's major money-spinner, with the current production of this 150mph (240kph) bespoke road racer running at around 3,000 units a year. More than 1,000 of these are snapped up by the US market.

THE M5

Although Garching is working to maximum capacity, at the time of writing there was still a six-month waiting list for the M5. 'It is a hand-made car,' says Sales Director Martin Hainge with some pride. 'If you want it in canary yellow with green hide upholstery, that is what you will get.'

However, if the marketing men offer a wide variety of trim and body colour, the customer has no choice as far as engine specification is concerned. There is only one specification and a fixed suspension configuration, although every power unit is bench-tested before receiving the final seal of approval.

A total of 150 technicians out of Motorsport's 475 workforce concentrate on the M5 manufacturing process. Trimmed 5-series bodyshells are delivered to Garching from BMW's main assembly lines at Dingolfing. The engines are sourced from a Munich plant devoted solely to the manufacture of the four-valve-per-cylinder engines and the V12s used in the 750i and 850i models.

It takes two men two-and-a-half hours to assemble the front suspension and engine into one unit, while two more take almost that time to build the rear-axle assembly. Each six-cylinder engine is bench-tested to ensure that it delivers the requisite 315bhp (310bhp for the US market models) and the

BMW's one female driver in 1991 was Annette Meeuvissen, who drove this M3 for the Linder team alongside Heger and Dieter Quester.

Prior to the M3's arrival, the 635CSi held the fort as BMW's front-line racing weapon in the mid-1980s.

leather trim is cut, stitched and fitted by hand while the car sits on an individual hoist.

Each M5 has its rear axle camber and castor adjustments carried out by computer in both laden and unladen conditions and, once the final assembly is completed, every car is taken on a 25-mile (40km) road test. Kalbfell recounts with some pleasure that around ten per cent of customers come to Garching to see their car being built.

The first seventy M5s for the Japanese market, in left-hand-drive trim, were exported in July 1991. These orders have been achieved despite rejecting demands from the Japanese and US markets for automatic transmission. Around 700 M5s go to the USA each year.

Meanwhile, ten technicians concentrate solely on assembling the M3 racing engines, taking advantage of six fully enclosed engine dynomometers on which the progress of their high-revving charges are monitored by television screens and digital read-outs. These dynos have the capacity to record up to 13,000rpm and 1,200bhp, but even that wasn't enough for the old 1.5-litre four-cylinder Formula 1 turbos, which were capable of flash readings of 1,500bhp before disintegrating!

Depending on demand, between fifty and 100 racing M3 engines are built each year. Seventeen engine designers are kept occupied on CAD/CAM stations, constantly probing for means of reducing their development time.

*Long-time BMW campaigner Dieter Quester, son-in-law of Alex von
Falkenhausen, took his fourth European Touring Car Championship title in
this 635CSi in 1983.*

NEW PROJECTS

At the start of 1991, BMW had three new
models in the pipeline, only two of which
were realistically destined to see the light of
day. The second-generation M3 will be
powered by a new multi-valve six-cylinder
engine – dubbed the M50 – of around 2.5-
litre capacity. This is expected to develop in
the order of 250bhp in road trim. Casting
aside the somewhat extrovert lines of the
original M3, the second generation model is
expected to feature only the most subtle
bodywork modifications and aerodynamic
aids. It will also have further uprated

suspension, wider wheels and tyres and
stronger brakes.

Next in the order of priorities is a more
powerful M5, equipped with a 3.9-litre version of the 24-valve straight-six which dates
back to the M1. Its big-bore engine is
expected to develop in the region of 350bhp.
This should be sufficient to deal with the
challenge of the equally specialist Mercedes-
Benz 500E. Also under preparation are 9in
wheel rims all round, BMW's ASC+T traction control device and a lighter body which
is expected to feature aluminium panels
where this is structurally feasible.

The most exciting contender of all in 1991

*These BMW promotional photographs, released in 1979, are of the BMW M1,
then the pride of the Motorsport operation. The functional, yet elegant,
Giugiaro-styled coupe still looks as fresh as tomorrow more than a decade later.*

opposition from the ranks of the owner-drivers. However, before the series got off the starting blocks, Procar would immediately encounter a few snags as the events at Zolder, over the weekend of the 1979 Belgian Grand Prix, were to prove.

At the end of the first Grand Prix qualifying sessions, the top five on the timing sheets were Gilles Villeneuve (Ferrari), Jean-Pierre Jabouille (Renault), Jacques Laffite (Ligier), Clay Regazzoni (Williams)

and Mario Andretti (Lotus). With the Procars running on Goodyear rubber, there was no way in which the Michelin-contracted Ferrari or Renault drivers could take part. In any case, the French national car company wasn't particularly interested in either of its drivers carrying out what amounted to unpaid promotional work for BMW!

As a result, it was necessary to trawl progressively further down the list of practice times. Next up was Ferrari driver Jody

Rearward visibility is in fact better than one might imagine, through the slatted rear body cover which is designed to duct hot air from the engine bay.

Keeping away from the kerbs. Henry on the Donington Park circuit with the M1 Procar.

I never checked whether these cars had come directly from Monaco with their cockpits adjusted for those F1 drivers who used them there, or whether they were prepared specially for the Donington stars. One thing's for certain; the seat designated for James Hunt was quite large enough for my rear end, so Stappert decreed that car number 20 — carrying the Olympus Wolf identification of James's F1 sponsors — would be the machine at risk. A quick try in the confined cockpit was enough to confirm that I would fit. And, in the event of a disaster (to me) there was always a spare Procar available (for Hunt).

Star Attraction

Procar. The most expensive one-make category in the world, unless the IROC organizers know otherwise. Drummed up by Jochen Neerpasch and Max Mosley, with FOCA blessing, this BMW M1 series was designed to expand the F1 package and get regular Grand Prix stars out in production racers once again.

The cynical would also remark that it got BMW Competitions out of an embarrassing corner with their unhomologated BMW coupes. Planned as a contender in the Group 5 'silhouette' category, a whole host of production problems threw the M1 schedule way behind time. The prospect of a well developed central-engined BMW coupe — turbocharged in due course — taking on the might of the Porsche empire, might have been one factor that could have saved international sports car racing from its present nadir.

Sadly, the car wasn't even ready for homologation even by the beginning of this year. Initially, lack of surplus capacity at BMW's existing plants meant that they had to look outside for an M1 assembly facility. Eventually, a deal was forged with Lamborghini, but this fell through almost before it had begun, only seven coupes being completed.

*Emerson Fittipaldi's M1 heads Patrick Depailler's machine on the opening lap
of the Procar event supporting the 1979 Monaco Grand Prix. The race was won
by Niki Lauda.*

To save the project, a deal was done with Bauer in Stuttgart where the M1s are now produced with engines supplied from Munich, bodies from Ital Design and gearboxes from ZF.

Given that they can't go sports car racing against 'Porsche and the others' the Procar series was devised. The cars are turned out to what might best be described as 'Unhomologated Group A' specification, but the format of the races has provoked yet another monumental row between FISA, the sport's governing body, and those behind the Procars (i.e. the Procar Association and FOCA). FISA have decreed that the BMW M1 series isn't a serious form of motor racing, merely a publicity exercise.

What's more, the French Federation has tried to ban them from racing at the French Grand Prix later this month. And, since Bernie Ecclestone has made it clear that there won't be a French Grand Prix if there isn't a Procar race . . . But that's another story!

The Procar cause has not been helped by opposition within the FOCA ranks, both from entrants and drivers. Commercial interests prevent the four drivers on Michelin from driving the Goodyear-shod M1s, while others feel that such a category shouldn't have its races mixed in with a Grand Prix programme. Ken Tyrrell has even expressed the view 'BMW should build an F1 car if they want to get in on Grand Prix racing . . .' To my mind, that view seems about as insular as you can get.

On the other hand, a large bag of gold from Marlboro and an immaculately prepared M1 from Project Four Racing ensures that twice World Champion Niki Lauda will be competing in every round of the Procar series – whether or not he qualifies as one of the star drivers. After an abysmal start at Zolder, where reliability was a big problem, the Procars produced really exciting racing round the tight confines of Monaco with Niki elbowing his way past Regazzoni with a lap-and-a-bit to go to snatch a narrow victory.

Mean Machine

Anyway, back to the M1 racer itself. With its flared arches, front air dam and full-width rear wing, the M1 looks an impressive and aggressive machine – even more so in the distinctive BMW 'house livery'. Beneath the beautifully finished fibreglass bodyshell is a spaceframe/sheet steel chassis powered by a 3,453cc straight-six engine. This is a derivative of the famous and versatile Gp 2 CSL unit which enjoyed so much success in the European Touring Car Championship. But as my colleague (and BMW expert) Jeremy Walton is quick to point out, the M1's engine is effectively a six-cylinder version of the F2 motor, complete with gear-driven overhead camshafts, bigger inlet and exhaust valves, revised camshaft profiles and Kugelfischer injection complete with racing pump.

Power output is around 470bhp at 9,000rpm, although the rev limiters on the Procars are set at 8,500rpm in the interests of reliability. However, with non-adjustable gear ratios, it's down to the driver not to run

Nelson Piquet heads for victory in the Gunnar Nilsson Memorial event at Donington Park, June 1979.

Battery and other ancillaries are mounted behind the water radiator (right) beneath the bonnet.

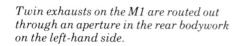

Twin exhausts on the M1 are routed out through an aperture in the rear bodywork on the left-hand side.

Tight squeeze: the 3.5-litre, 24-valve BMW six in the M1's engine bay.

The distinctive bumper line is extended through the door and rear bodywork to accentuate the M1's squat profile.

less exploitive intention. Back in the late seventies BMW's Motorsports boss Jochen Neerpasch wanted a car to replace the ageing and flagging bewinged CSL on the race tracks of the world. The main requirements were that it would be potent enough to take on the then-dominant Porsches in Group 4 and have the potential to mix it in Group 5 (silhouette) racing.

Desperately Seeking Supercar

Neerpasch quickly realized that what he needed wasn't another CSL, but a serious mid-engined supercar. Moreover, he needed at least 400 examples for homologation in Group 4 fast. An obvious contrast with Honda's cost-no-object brief emerged; because it would have disrupted BMW's mainstream programme to divert energy into the design, development and production of the M1, Neerpasch was forced to look elsewhere for help. And where better to sub-contract a supercar than in the homeland of supercars, Italy? The main decisions were quickly made. Ital Design would do the body, Lamborghini the chassis design, overall development and final assembly. Power? Perfect as it would have been, BMW's already-mooted 4-litre V12 was a long way from becoming a reality so a 24-valve version of the existing straight-six with close on 300bhp got the job.

The man with the job of guaranteeing the M1 an astounding aesthetic impact was Giugiaro. The fact that the shape he created looks, if anything, better now than it did then says as much about the great stylist's subsequent international influence in this field as the cool brilliance of the original design.

A handful of prototypes as dramatic as anything from the Emilian plains was spawned by BMW and Lamborghini's unusual alliance in the early months.

design from the seventies that's hardest to ignore. The BMW M1 – a famous BMW to be sure, but a sorely underrated supercar.

Unlike Honda, it wasn't BMW's intention to sanction the best and most drivable supercar a big budget and a battery of number-crunching Cray computers to create. It was sired from a much simpler and, if you like,

Safety was a hallmark

The car which spawned the BMW M1, the Paul Bracq-designed 1972 BMW Turbo, was regarded by its makers as a machine which also demonstrated the Munich company's overriding commitment to safety, as Eric Dymock explains succinctly in *BMW – A Celebration*:

Bracq's prototype had been constructed by Michelotti in Turin and was intended as a riposte to the vogue for Experimental Safety Vehicles (ESVs). Far from being tank-like, the BMW Turbo as it was known, used as 2002 four-cylinder with a turbocharger, and had deformable structures and a jointed steering column, together with a strong roll-over bar to achieve what was known in the post-Nader jargon as passive safety.

Yet BMW stood out for active safety, that is to say providing the driver with the best means of actively avoiding an accident rather than passively sitting waiting for it. Accordingly, the car was equipped with anti-lock brakes, still something of a novelty, and its mid-engined configuration, designed to provide the best possible weight distribution, gave increased safety through superior handling.

On the subject of the M1 racing programme in general, Dymock continues:

On the credit side, the result (the M1) was an outstanding road car, every bit as remarkable as the 328 of the 1930s, and it did demonstrate that when it came to state-of-the-art automotive engineering, BMW had the talent and the resources to make the best.

Some of the BMW management were miffed at what they regarded as the failure of the Silhouette formula to happen, but it was manifestly not Neerpasch's fault. The category had become a casualty of the convoluted politics of motor racing, and not only BMW, but also other manufacturers, learned a good deal from the experience.

Lamborghini's highly regarded chassis ace, Ing. Dallara, had an input from the start and said plenty about the exceptional properties of Pirelli's then-new P7 tyre gained from his experience with the similarly shod Countach. At this stage, there was every reason for Neerpasch to feel optimistic about the M1's progress. The Bavarian beauty was shaping up well; its sharp appearance and evident speed were hot gossip in Munich and Sant 'Agata alike.

Sant 'Agata Blues

But big trouble was coming. Out of the blue, Lamborghini's money dried up. The £1.1 million lent by the Italian government for component funding and assembly was all gone before a single M1 had been produced. By this time BMW was in too deep to abort the project. Lamborghini, however, was out for the count. It could have been worse, but not much. The component suppliers Lamborghini had signed up were willing (probably delighted) to continue, but a relatively unknown engineering outfit run by the brothers Marchesi was entrusted with the welding of the square-section spaceframe chassis, while glassfibre specialists TIR supplied the panels. In a deal which makes the Seat Ibiza's multi-sourced design look like a model of homogenity, Ital Design agreed to mate bodies with chassis at its own premises and the Stuttgart-based coachbuilder Bauer handled final assembly.

And finally the M1 did go on sale – in February 1979, a year later than intended. It didn't look rushed, the specification appeared uncompromised and it was unquestionably exotic. Its torsionally strong square-section steel spaceframe was clothed entirely in unstressed panels and, as already mentioned, the car ran on 205/55 VR16 (front) and 225/50 VR16 Pirelli P7s on 7 and 8in alloy rims. These, in turn, supported alloy hub carriers located by unequal length wishbones with pronounced anti-dive/squat geometry.

The registration number says it all. This M1 was owned by the enthusiastic Tim Willson of Cheylsmore Garages, who also supported BMW driver Christian Danner during his Formula 3000 programme in 1985.

The rear-view of the M1.

The lockable filler cap is not recessed, calling for some care when replenishing the M1's tank

The instrumentation and switchgear were borrowed from the 6-series coupe.

A combination of graceful, well-balanced lines, deep spoilers and purposeful low-profile rubber makes the M635CSi a covetable possession – even before sampling its prodigious performance.

BMW was always hot on graphic liveries for its racing saloons. This is the Schnitzer-prepared 635CSi, which took third place in the 1986 Spa 24-hour endurance race.

Photo finish for the Schnitzer BMWs at Spa with car no. 11, shared by Dieter Quester, Altfried Heger and Thierry Tassin taking victory and the no. 10 car of Roberto Ravaglia, Gerhard Berger and Emanuele Pirro finishing third.

Of course, this was in the days before Sir John Egan began to shake Jaguar into some sort of competitive shape from the viewpoint of build quality. At that time, just over £15,000 spent on an XJ-S was something of a major gamble.

At the time, I was editing *Motor Sport*'s stablemate, the weekly newspaper *Motoring News,* and we had been afforded the opportunity to road test the 635CSi some six months ahead of our colleagues on the monthly.

I had already reached the conclusion that the BMW was undoubtedly worth the £5,000-odd premium that would have had to be spent to bring the 635 up to the equipment level offered by the basic Jaguar. And this even though BMW's price structure when it came to extras was, and still is, irksome as far as accurately cross-referencing their costs in comparison with rival models is concerned.

*Dark colour schemes show off
M635CSi in an elegantly
understated light.*

*Line of wrap-round bumpers is
continued by rubber protective strip
mid-way up the doors.*

Discreet white-on-black 170mph (274kph) speedometer falls easily within the driver's eye-line.

Electric seat adjustment and programme switches on the side of the driver's seat squab.

in the same price league as the Ferrari Mon-
dial, Lamborghini Jalpa, Mercedes 420SEC
and, of course, right in the middle of 911
territory. The M6 is roomier than all but the
Mercedes and potent enough to embarrass
many of its more overtly sporting rivals.

Under Cover

Open the bonnet and the reason is obvious.
BMW MPower is the legend on the crackle
black cam cover. Beneath are twin camshafts
and the 24 valves to boost power from the
standard 635CSi's 220bhp at 5,700rpm to
286bhp at 6,500rpm. Torque is increased,
too, from 232lb/ft at 4,000rpm to 251lb/ft at
4,500rpm.

But MPower means more than a multi-
valve head. There's a stouter crank with 2mm
shorter stroke, longer con rods, and stronger,
high compression pistons in a 1.4mm larger
bore block. This gives a capacity of 3,453cc, a
slight increase over the single cam engine.
Manifolding is changed too, but both engines
share Bosch Motronic mapped fuel injection
and ignition. A beefier clutch feeds an
increased output to a ZF close-ratio, five-
speed manual gearbox.

The changes from standard specification
don't end there. A limited slip differential
and massive 240/45 Michelins keep each
wheel firmly clamped to the tarmac, while
firmer suspension settings and a lower stance
add further to cornering capabilities. Braking is taken care of by huge discs all round
with huge four-pot racing calipers.

At small throttle openings there is little
indication of the huge performance available.
The big BMW glides along on just a whiff of
throttle in top gear. Change down and floor
the throttle, though, and the M6's character
is transformed. There's a squawk from the
hefty Michelins as they grip the tarmac, the
nose rises with a sense of purpose and the
BMW's great bulk shoots forward.

There's no peakiness in the power delivery,
just an overwhelming gain in momentum
backed up by the hard-edged mechanical
howl from the engine, the whine or hard-
worked transmission gears meshing
together, and an urgent exhaust wail.

Facts and Figures

Performance figures back up the subjective
impressions. From rest, 60mph comes up in
just 6secs – an exceptional time for a front
engined car. Change into third and, at
100mph, only 15.1secs have elapsed.

In-gear figures are equally impressive.
Third gear is the best overtaking ratio in
most conditions, each 20mph increment from
40 to 90mph taking around 4secs. Fourth
carries the big BMW all the way to 130mph
before a change into top is necessary.

The car feels rock steady at maximum
speed with little more than the roar of the
wind for company. The maximum of 150mph
has the big engine turning over at 6,200rpm,
just below peak power in fact.

The BMW's brakes are reassuringly powerful and free from fade. The weighting is
just right with no sudden response in gentle
use and a firm, progressive action.

While never quiet, the 24-valver always
feels smooth and potent, though power comes
on much stronger beyond 3,500rpm. Fine
mechanical smoothness is enhanced by a
beautifully progressive throttle linkage.

Considering the terrific performance of the
M6, fuel economy is a pleasant surprise. The
overall figure of 20.6mpg gives a range of
about 300 miles on one tankful. Motorway
driving hiked the overall figure to 23.5mpg
while, remarkably, even during performance
testing the consumption never dropped below
17mpg.

The M635CSi has impeccable road manners. Outright grip and traction are simply
outstanding. Thankfully, BMW's engineers
spare us the Servotronic steering fitted to the
7-series, opting instead for the weightier
recirculating ball arrangement.

A bootful of throttle in a tight bend will

The near-identical 635CSi and latest M5 six-cylinder engine on display in the foyer at BMW Motorsport headquarters.

unstick the back end. On a wet or greasy road, restraint is essential. But the M6 is so well balanced that applying the right amount of corrective lock seems to come naturally. High-speed sweepers, for example, induce nothing more than mild understeer – you really do need to push hard to provoke anything beyond on-rails handling.

By contrast, ride refinement is not a strong point. Compared with the supple ride of the regular 635CSi, the M-badged car lacks subtlety. It feels as though everything has been stiffened up for the sake of good handling with scant regard for ride quality or road noise suppression. This is quite deliberate.

When worked hard the engine gets noisy, too, though at cruising speeds it settles down to a subdued thrum. Then it is the wind roar that intrudes, mostly from around the sunroof and

the frameless door windows. But on abrasive and concrete surfaces, tyre rumble competes with wind roar as the worst offender.

Inside Information

Inside, the M6 has a full leather interior, stitched from enough hides to clothe a small herd – 27 square metres in all. The quality, style and finish are tasteful and classy.

The driving position is basically fine with nicely set pedals inviting heel and toe gearchanges, a conveniently positioned gear lever and a range of powered seat adjustments that

(Overleaf)BMW's 5-litre V12-engined M8 prototype was a Motorsport prestige confection which failed to get the green light for production.

Deep frontal spoiler and BMW Motorsport
stripes give distinctive external identity to
the first M535i, based on the first generation
5-series shell.

Cosmetic changes to the first 5-series
bodyshell signalled the arrival of the M-Series
◄ road car identification.

Rear boot spoiler on the M535i was a crucial
factor for high-speed stability.

BMW M535i (1980)

ENGINE

Block material	Cast iron
Head material	Aluminium alloy
Cylinders	In-line six
Cooling	Water
Bore and stroke	93.4 × 84mm
Capacity	3,453cc
Main bearings	Seven
Valves	4 per cylinder; dohc
Compression ratio	9.3:1
Max. power	218bhp at 5,200rpm
Max. torque	228lb/ft at 4,000rpm

TRANSMISSION

Clutch	
Type	5-speed Getrag manual

OVERALL GEAR RATIOS

Top	1.01
4th	1.236
3rd	1.766
2nd	2.403
1st	3.717
Reverse	
Final drive	3.07

SUSPENSION AND STEERING

Front	Inclined coil spring struts with Bilstein shock absorbers and rubber anti-roll bar
Rear	Auxiliary springs; trailing arms with Bilstein spring/damper. Anti-roll bar
Steering	Recirculatory ball, power assisted
Tyres	Michelin 195/70 VR14 radials
Wheels	Mahle-BBS 6½ × 14 alloy

BRAKES

Type	Ventilated discs front, solid rear. Vacuum servo

DIMENSIONS

Length	4,620mm
Width	1,690mm
Height	1,425mm
Wheelbase	2,636mm
Track (F/R)	1,420/1,460mm
Turning circle	10.5m

There really doesn't seem to be a power curve, as such, though from 3,500 to 5,500rpm there's enough eagerness to satisfy all but the most bloodthirsty pilot. I must confess, together with my co-pilot, to driving up to the limit of 6,000rpm quite regularly. We even managed 6,000rpm and indicated 140mph in top for a couple of miles, just to see how stable and how rapid this car was. More practical is the way in which this BMW will lope between 70 and 120mph equably.

All the important qualities, retardation, steering and cornering ability are in a league that the normal 5-series owner might find hard to recognize. The steering is endowed with uncanny stability in cross-winds because of front and rear spoilers, the brakes and suspension changes equally effective . . .

Comfort has certainly not been neglected with central locking, tinted glass, a sunroof, the usual variable ratio ZF power steering and electrically operated mirrors as standard items. The spoilers are a no-cost option, but the air conditioning will be a substantially priced extra; like the rest of the car, it is very effective in a modest way.

Surely this apparent paragon has faults. A heavy clutch combined with awkward first to second movement detracts from the easy way the 535i wafts through urban motoring. This driver also managed under 17mpg, but since the rest of those assessing the car managed 23–24mpg and still enjoyed the extra performance, I feel that 20mpg, an independently tested figure, is a fair average and a creditable one for a 3½-litre bulky saloon. It is not that much lighter than the 6-series coupe.

M535i, 1985–1987

Despite being introduced in April 1981, it was not until 1984 that the second generation 5-series bodyshell came in for the same treatment and another M-badged 535i was introduced – a total of 9,483 examples of this 218bhp machine being produced through until December 1987. Comparing this machine with the first generation M535i was a pretty meaningless exercise, as the earlier car was much lower geared. Besides, most people regarded the yardstick by which the new car was to be measured as the 528i saloon which had also been metamorphosed into the second generation bodyshell.

This latest machine – only the second saloon to carry the M-series identification, but in reality nothing more than an exercise in badge engineering – produced a top speed of 143mph (218kph) from its 218bhp version of the smooth BMW six, demonstrating the same glorious flexibility and smoothness which characterized the M5.

However, the M535i was prone to the rear subframe vibration that had evidently been cured on the M5. In addition, the ZF-gearbox, which it inherited from the 528i, had first gear dog-legged to the left with reverse placed immediately ahead of it, and the spring guarding reverse far too weak. Road testers reported that it was all too easy to snag reverse while making a fast change from first to second.

That said, the wide-ratio box was more than sufficient to deal with the additional torque developed by the M535i (229lb/ft at 4,000rpm). BMW considered that the 528i's existing 11.2in (284mm) diameter discs, ventilated at the front, provided sufficient retardation to deal with the extra 34bhp delivered by the M535i. But wider 220/55VR390 Michelin TRXs replaced the 200/60VR390 tyres fitted to the 2.8-litre car and the later machine's aerodynamic penetration was enhanced by the incorporation of a deep front air dam, sill extensions to slightly shield the wheels and, as a legacy of the original M353i, a boot lid extending lip service.

Suspension changes over the 528i were limited to slightly uprated springs and the fitting of gas-filled dampers to the

Clever M-series striping gives first-generation 5-series saloon a somewhat garish look.

The leather-rimmed sports steering wheel dominated M535i controls.

Hip-hugging Recaro seats were standard equipment for front occupants.

The first of the bespoke M5s was produced between 1985 and 1988 round the second generation 5-series bodyshell. It had no competition application, but packaged racetrack performance for road use.

Autocar
6 March 1985

Michael Scarlett

It is true that . . . ambling along at 1,000rpm in fifth at 24mph I am able to ease out and past the obstruction without changing down, that from the outside the 800rpm idle has a ponderous note, heavier than usual. But there is nothing rorty, nothing crude, above all nothing show-off, about this 5-series car.

Then the 80kph near-city limit on the autobahn south to Garmisch Partenkirchen ends, and the new BMW-designed, Getrag-machined gearbox is double-declutched into third and the right foot flattened. Instantly, my back is shoved into the seat and I am cursing mildly as the rev limiter cuts in at 2,000rpm before the 6,900rpm red line, at 96mph – not that it really matters. Fourth is a sweet snatch back through the conventional touring-type gate and I'm in that only a short time before easing the short lever into the fifth dog-leg, at 130mph, just on the 6,700rpm effective limit.

The discreet M-Sport flashes on the lower steering wheel spoke is the only real giveaway that this interior is of no run-of-the-mill BMW.

M5 identification extends to the message on the door sills.

High-quality leather-trimmed bucket front seats highlight the interior of the first M5.

The deep rear skirt enhances the squared-off rear view of the M5.

Square-rigged and unobtrusive, the first M5 hardly shouted out its identity.

The high-powered twin headlamp set-up features integral wash-wipe facility.

The M5's 286bhp six-cylinder endowed this outwardly unassuming saloon with a 150mph-plus capability.

Magical designation for connoisseurs of performance motoring.

Cross-spoked alloy wheels were the biggest clue to M5's true potential

High-quality leather trim extends to interior door pulls and panelling.

First M5 spoiler wrapped gently round its boot-lid top.

There is, relatively speaking, a little more time to consider the noise of this 24-valve, 3,453cc double overhead camshaft six as the car accelerates towards its maximum speed. There is that lovely BMW straight-six rising yowl you hear on the cooking engines – if that is a fair label for such still-exciting power units – but with a deeper, harder note, a kind of crying growl on full song which dominates the small amount of wind noise and average road noise, but is nothing but music played at the right volume.

On the Road

The motorway stays clear, there is virtually no wind, and the speedometer steadies at 252kph (nearly 157mph); the stopwatch clicks over one, then two kilometres at an average of 14.32sec per km – 153mph. Got to do the job properly, so we turn round at the next ausfahrt, wait for the right chance, and go. Result over the opposite direction same stretch – a timed 152.8mph, giving a mean 152.9 at 6,400rpm, very close to the 6,500 peak at which the ex-M1 engine's 282bhp occurs. An important, if minor, indication of how everything about this car is done properly, by men of engineering good taste.

No, it's not quiet, and on one's way up to decent speeds, again on the occasions when a little knot of traffic slows one, there is a marked heterodyne between 4,800 and 5,100 in fifth, and the ride is on the firm side, if still acceptable. But there is nothing loud about the M5 acoustically or otherwise; it doesn't even have the M535i's boot lip extension, and the slightly deepened front air dam is done subtly, yet stability at top speed is reassuring.

Off the motorway, north of the Austrian border, a standing start is tried for fun and, as the 220/55VR390 TRXs spin at the back, it is interesting to find none of the usual BMW rear subframe judder. The 25 per cent limited slip differential makes the tyres squeak on tight manoeuvring. Ambling very slowly, the flexibility of the engine is outstanding;

you can accelerate without discomfort from 600rpm in fifth, although the usual over-run cut-off jerkiness spoils things above 1,200rpm, below which injection and ignition are restored.

Opening Up

Time to stop and look under the bonnet. One of the pleasures of owning an exciting car should be just the look of what's under the nose (or tail) – and this BMW does not disappoint. That great length of broad black-crackle and bright-aluminium cam cover is crammed in, just, with an inch clearance at the bulkhead end, and another between the cover over the exhaust-camshaft-driven electronic ignition distributor and the radiator in front, its top bearing a nice piece of engine builder's swank – BMW M-POWER in big cast letters.

Another piece of intended swank – the numbers 24-6 cast onto the inlet tract air box – misses the bus, as the radiator expansion tank partly hides it. This great engine leans to the right, making the cobra's nest of tubular exhaust manifolding weaving among itself tightly snuggled under.

Bavarian country roads don't encourage ultimate experiments with handling, but the car feels as if it will behave like its officially approved Alpina cousins, controllably. Its brakes are ideal, not too light, yet highly effective, backed up of course with Bosch's four channel Anti-Blockier-System which copes contemptuously with mixed surfaces on each side; dry road left, melting snow right.

What is an M5? Why M5, which is a departure from normal BMW nomenclature – if you forget the now dead M1? Briefly, as explained at its Amsterdam Show launch, it is the work of BMW Motorsport GmbH, a connoisseur's car, which will be made at no more than 250 per annum, costing a base 80,750DM in Germany against roughly 50,000DM for the normal production M535i.

It is much more of a bespoke order machine;

you can, within the limits of suitability, pay for whatever specification fitting details you wish. An example exclusive to the M5 is that seats, door panels, centre console and hand-brake lever can be upholstered in natural buffalo hide leather. Another is the radio equipment; the car I tried had an elaborate Becker Mexico set with extra amplifier. Presumably, those of an exhibitionist turn of mind can have the thing made as gaudy as they like – but it would miss the point.

BMW Motorsport is keen to be the sort of commercial success that Ford's SVE department is – Formula 1 engines are not cheap – and so it isn't surprising to hear mutterings about a line of M-Cars, with an M3 coming later, powered by another, part-new, four-valves-per cylinder six. It is working on a right-hand-drive M5, but with all 250 LHD cars already ordered for 1985, this won't appear for some time. It is more than worth waiting for.

THE NEW 5-SERIES RANGE

For 1988, BMW introduced a completely new 5-series saloon which was visually closely identifiable with the V12-engined 7-series that had come on to the market some fifteen months before. Whereas the old 5-series had looked traditionally angular, the new car sported a subtly aerodynamic profile which produced a slightly reduced drag coefficient.

By 1988, the second generation M5 had burst on to the scene. It combined the performance levels achieved by the M1 with docility and high standards of accommodation.

The frontal view offers M5 badging on the grille, but wide 8J × 17 front rims spell ultra-high performance.

The latest M5, built round the third generation 5-series bodyshell, continues the theme of Motorsport's understated style. At first glance, only the wheels say this is no normal 5-series saloon.

£27,000 worth of difference?' Anybody taking a cursory glance through the magazine would perhaps have been surprised to discover that the answer, displayed in the sub-heading, was in the negative. That said, there was no doubt that they rated the M5 as 'the most accomplished saloon car ever made'. Many people would come to share their views.

As Editor Bob Murray noted, he found some difficulty understanding why several of his magazine's rivals found it hard to pigeon-hole the car. He concluded that it was simply a stunning example of hand-made craftsmanship. Referring to it figuratively as 'the world's greatest Sierra', he was not seeking to decry the M5's achievements. His point was merely that BMW had successfully imbued a full four-door saloon with Ferrari-like standards of performance and roadholding.

The M5, he concluded, had the highest top speed, the best through-the-gears acceleration, the best handling/ride compromise and the best performance/economy ratio of any car with the ability to transport four adults and their luggage. He mirrored the widely held view that this second-generation M5 was less raunchy and overtly sporting than its predecessor, but only in the sense that it delivered shattering levels of performance and grip without any displays of temperament or compromise on comfort.

Standard equipment on the M5 included a fair swathe of creature comforts, including ABS anti-lock brakes, electric windows, power-assisted steering, active check control, on-board computer, the limited slip differential, electric sports seats, self-levelling suspension, electric sunroof, headlight washers and air conditioning. It was available only with a five-speed manual gearbox and, in the first year, only 260 right-hand-drive examples would be made available for UK customers. The first deliveries for British customers were scheduled for April 1991 and, with dealers having already taken 350 orders

by the previous November, it was clearly destined to be a machine in short supply.

At first acquaintance some testers reached the conclusion that whatever improvements there had been to the torque curve, they were not quite enough. There was an absence of strong performance below 3,500rpm which left one wondering just how much more agile the car might be if it weighed 500lb (225kg) less. However, that was only part of the overall story, as Bob Murray recounted in *Autocar & Motor*. He takes up the story.

Autocar & Motor
12 September 1990

Bob Murray

That the engine recoups any ground lost at low revs is beyond question, for it goes on to provide a breathtaking combination of performance and refinement over a wide rev range. It starts to get really businesslike at 4,250rpm and ends at 7,000rpm only because the soft cushion of the rev limiter insists on it. The delivery is impeccable, the response clean and quick, the six-cylinder wail a constant if muted incitement to delve ever deeper into this formidable engine's reserves. Coupled with a beautifully tight drive train and good gear ratios, any exploration of the engine's upper reaches is pure joy.

And on the track it indeed does the business: 0–60mph in 6.4sec, 0–100 in 15.6, the standing quarter mile in 15 dead at 98mph, 30–70mph through the gears in 5.7sec. And this despite the test car's rev limiter cutting in a good couple of hundred revs before the red line. As with all BMWs, top speed is restricted to the 150kmph mark, and since our best of 158mph falls a little short of peak power revs it certainly is a restriction, though there would only ever be another 5 to 6mph available without it. The M5 could probably pull 7,000 in fifth for 163mph, but I can't

M5 identification on door sills.
Also note the electric seat adjustment
controls for fore/aft movement
and back-rest angling.

Unique two-part wheels include
outer radial blades producing
axial effect to direct cooling
air on to brake discs.

The electric steel sliding sunroof
comes as part of the M5's basic
package.

An all-leather interior is an optional extra on the M5, but hand-stitched to perfection by BMW Motorsport.

The deep spoiler gives the frontal aspect of the M5 a well-rounded, undramatic appearance.

The ultimate derivative of the M1 engine; BMW's latest M5 produces a lusty 315bhp from this silky smooth 3,535cc unit.

imagine anyone caring. More to the point; the gearing is perfect.

Rivals

Performance comparisons? You must look to the exotic names to find them, and then all with the exception of the Bentley Turbo R are two-door cars and only two-plus-two seating at best.

The Bentley, automatic of course, loses on top speed and the 30–70mph test but otherwise is pretty close. The serious Lotuses, Ferraris, Lamborghinis and Porsches all have the M5's measure, but it's interesting to note that this Bavarian Q-car is more than a match for the Aston Martin Virage in all but one area: fourth and fifth gear flexibility, where the British V8 has the expected advantage, though it is not as great as you might expect from the BMW's apparent flatness low down. There's only a second and a bit between them from 30–50mph in top gear, so the BMW is certainly deceptive in this regard. They weigh about the same, too. In second and third gears, the M5 is always ahead of the Virage.

This extraordinary performance for a saloon is not at the expense of an inordinate thirst. Our overall consumption of 19mpg is first class, especially as it allows a fine touring range of 400 miles from the 90-litre (19.8gal) tank.

The M5's handling strengths weren't shown to best advantage in our Castle Combe handling extravaganza earlier this year – too much understeer, too little adjustability – but that didn't stop it posting lap times second only to the Caterham 7 HPC. The car's timeless performance that day – braking stamina in particular was impossible to fault – impressed us all, but it did only hint at what a well driven M5 can achieve on the road.

Repertoire

Quite a repertoire it is too, far from perfect in all areas, true, but overall as capable a package as ever had 315bhp to deal with. The net result is that 315 horses surely never felt so manageable – so often usable – as in this car. Roadholding, braking power and suspension and body control, unquestionably take production saloon car standards several notches higher. The chassis is balanced and, more importantly, you know it is by the messages through your backside. You can play with this car in corners, pushing the nose wide with mild understeer or bringing it back in to the apex and letting the tail drift a bit – all is possible. And all is superbly controllable thanks to the genuinely benign breakaway characteristics of the Michelin tyres.

They are perhaps not as sharp as the optional Pirellis, but they do work very well with the chassis for truly forgiving and exploitable handling – on wet or dry roads. There's no traction control system here, but then even on those wet roads the car never feels in need of it.

The steering and brake-pedal feel and the gearchange do not help the M5's cause. Some others have pitched their criticisms higher than this – combining the elements to come to the conclusion that the car lacks driver involvement. These people must have numb backsides if they think that. Nevertheless, communication through the thick-rimmed leather wheel is at a premium, and it is notably lifeless with more free play than you'd expect at the straight ahead position, even though straight tracking on motorways is good. It's ideally geared too, and precise. What it doesn't have is any inspiration factor.

For this sort of car, the brake-pedal feel is horrible, with a woolly initial travel that is no reassurance at all when closing rapidly on a downhill hairpin at full chat in third. Any (hydropneumatic) Citroën brake pedal is the best in my book with the Porsche 911's a close runner up – surely they can't be that hard to emulate?

And then there's the gearchange, which feels exactly like any BMW's. It is a lovely *thing to stroke between ratios when cruising through a town in your 320i, but quite inappropriate in a car of the M5's nature, and a complete mismatch with what is a very heavy, if smooth, clutch. The change needs to be shorter, heavier and with much stronger cross-gate springing.*

Pros and Cons

The M5's ride is a revelation. No car with anywhere near this performance has the same small-bump absorption; the suspension aspect that causes cars – even Sportpack Jaguars – to jar over ridges and motorway expansion joints. That the M5 soaks them up without harshness – and indeed without intrusive bump-thump or tyre roar, Porsche please note – is excellent, but it is not without a penalty. And there can be no denying that at three-figure speed the M5 doesn't feel as rooted to the road as much as, say, a 928. Never loose or floaty, but equally never as invincible feeling. Overall, it is a ride you could easily live with every day. I know; the Mercedes 300E-24 I do live with every day doesn't ride half as well.

And then, of course, there are all those things you just know BMW has got right; the perfect driving position and ergonomics, the fabulous seats (both front and back, and there really is room for four) and the low overall noise levels, though the test car's driver's window was sucked off its seals past

140mph, leading to an appalling increase in wind noise. The windscreen wipers, demisting functions, headlights, trip computer, stereo system and host of details, from a rearview mirror that automatically dips to watch the kerb when you select reverse gear to a vast range of cabin storage facilities, are a good cut above the ordinary. Incidentally, the console conceals a huge draw, gas-strut mounted, that feels better put together than some entire cars.

It's not all good news here, though. That wind noise problem, one-off though it may be, is inexcusable in a car of this cost, while the test car had enough other warts – constantly dropping-down sun visor, steering column fouling the shroud and hardly consistent rear door panel gaps – to indeed confirm that much of the car was put together by people rather than robots. Without any tangible benefit of Motorsport's hand assembly – why would anyone leave the ugly switch blanks on the dash or the bri-nylon look headlining? – it is rather too easy to question the worth of such specialized production. For the money this car needs to be pretty perfect.

It's not, of course. But, for my money, the other magazines moved the goalposts. And that the M5 missed scoring with them says more about them than the M5.

The simple reality is that this is the most accomplished saloon car ever made. And don't think for a moment it's not good fun.

7 The Versatile M3

The BMW M3 would become the most successful machine to carry the M-series derivation, selling in excess of 12,000 examples during a three-year production run which finished at the end of 1990. Based on the second generation 3-series machine – a highly successful commodity in its own right – the M3 fulfilled two crucial roles. On the one hand it sustained BMW's reputation for offering the enthusiastic motorist a small, specialist high performance saloon. On the other hand, it was tailored to enable the Munich company to reassert itself in both rallying and production car racing, at a time when the Formula 1 turbo programme was starting to lose some of its momentum.

The early 1980s had been marked by a considerable shift of emphasis as far as the European Touring Car Championship was concerned. BMW's traditional preserve for more than a decade had been gradually taken over by the Tom Walkinshaw-developed Jaguar XJS coupes, against which BMW had been obliged to field Group A racing versions of its 528i saloon. Developing approximately 240bhp from the outset, the 528i took Helmut Kelleners and Umberto Grano to the Drivers' title in the 1982 European Touring Car Championship.

However, with only around 240bhp at their disposal, they were simply not able to get on terms with the V12 Jaguars, so a revised version of the 635CSi coupe was developed in association with Schnitzer for the 1983 season. They were still not fully competitive with Jaguars but proved sufficiently consistent over a season to take Dieter Quester to his fourth European Touring Car title. But Jaguar took the title in 1984 and the turbo Volvo 240 followed this

up by grabbing overall honours the following year.

By 1986, Rover's SD1 V8 was into its final season of racing, scheduled for replacement at the end of the season, and beat its 635CSi opposition to the ETC Manufacturers' title, although Roberto Ravaglia took the drivers' crown. By this time, Jaguar had withdrawn as Walkinshaw concentrated his efforts on laying the groundwork for a Jaguar challenge in the Sports Car World Championship. Volvo also faded away, leaving Ford's newly developed Sierra Cosworth as the machine to beat. It was now a question of judging what BMW could produce which would be best suited to handling this formidable new challenge.

THE HOMOLOGATION CHALLENGE

The Group A regulations under which the European Touring Car Championship was now run demanded that 5,000 cars had to be manufactured to fulfil the qualifying homologation requirements. BMW Motorsport gave serious consideration to developing a 24-valve M635CSi, but it was quite evident that there was no way in which this machine could reach the production targets necessary to qualify. As a result, a clean sheet approach was adopted by the staff in Munich.

The concept of a serious competition car based round the 3-series bodyshell had been anticipated originally as early as 1981, but it was not until 1986 that the M3 finally made its bow. The chassis engineering was carried out by a design team under the

The M3 four-cylinder engine firmly advertised its competition pedigree.

BMW as 'being bad for the series', as the domination of a single manufacturer was not what FISA had desired.

Thomas Ammerschlager's design team had produced an out-and-out racing machine in the Division Two 2.4-litre M3, a highly developed and competitive car which had benefited from considerable pre-season testing, a lot of which was carried out at Mugello. The WTC team boasted reigning touring car champion Roberto Ravaglia, March Formula 1 driver Ivan Capelli, Formula 1 hopeful Emanuele Pirro and Austrian Roland Ratzenberger.

(Previous page) *Higher boot and more sloping rear roof-line are the most obvious hallmarks of the M3 as compared with a regular 3-series saloon.*

There was also a parallel European Touring Car Championship, but that turned out to be little more than a poorly supported farce. Ford were not competing with their Sierra Cosworth, with the result that works BMW M3 driver Winni Vogt had an easy run to overall victory.

Like BMW, Ford was determined to concentrate on the World Touring Car Championship through the efforts of the Swiss Eggenberger team. However, their season began badly with the Sierras excluded before the Italian race, due to some confusion over their engine management systems.

The M3s, one of which had been tried in practice by former triple World Champion Niki Lauda in his briefly held role as a

BMW M3 Group A

ENGINE

Block material	Iron
Head material	Aluminium alloy
Cylinders	In-line four
Cooling	Water
Bore and stroke	93.4 × 84mm
Capacity	2,302cc
Valves	4 per cylinder; dohc
Compression ratio	10.5:1
Fuel delivery system	Motronic fuel injection and engine management system
Max. power	320bhp at 8,200rpm
Max. torque	

TRANSMISSION

Clutch	Hydraulic
Type	Getrag 5-speed manual

OVERALL GEAR RATIOS

Top	1.00
4th	1.150
3rd	1.358
2nd	1.681
1st	2.337
Reverse	2.660
Final drive	From 3.15 to 5.28 variable

SUSPENSION AND STEERING

Front	MacPherson strut, twin tube dampers and anti-roll bar. Adjustable spring plates for varying vehicle height. Camber/castor adjustment
Rear	Semi-trailing arms, twin tube dampers and anti-roll bar. Adjustable spring plates for varying vehicle height adjustment. Camber/castor adjustment
Steering	Rack and pinion
Tyres	Michelin 225/45 VR16 MXX
Wheels	Cast light alloy 7.5J × 16

BRAKES

Type	Internally ventilated fix-caliper discs (front), solid discs (rear). ABS and servo. Integral handbrake drum

DIMENSIONS

Wheelbase	2,565mm
Track (F/R)	1,412/1,424mm
Length	4,345mm
Width	1,680mm
Height (unloaded)	1,370mm
Turning circle	12.1m

The most refined homologation special?
BMW's M3 combined widened arches and
aerodynamic spoilers to splendid aesthetic
effect.

BMW's 2.3-litre four-cylinder owed much to
the company's successful Formula 2 racing
units from the mid-1970s.

The centrally positioned rev counter
dominates the M3 fascia, emphasizing its
competition purpose.

BMW's M3 national racing team crowd round their 1987 Group A racing contender.

The M3s of Harald Grohs (leading) and Eric van de Poele battling for German Championship points at Hockenheim.

Clean lines with hood down. The action of electric motor transforms the package into fully enclosed trim.

Full skirting enhances the M3 convertible's overall proportions.

Markus Oesterich was amongst the fastest of BMW's youngsters during the 1987 season at the wheel of this Linder team M3.

M3 versus Sierra Cosworth: the essence of Group A saloon car racing in 1987.

The BMW M3 Sport Evolution arrived on the scene in 1990, allowing a slightly more powerful 2.5-litre engine and adjustable aerofoils to be homologated into Group A.

Based on the M3 Evolution, it featured the earlier car's front and rear spoilers and lighter rear body panels.

This commemorative BMW was offered with a wide range of luxury equipment, including a unique interior designed specifically by BMW Motorsport GmbH. Seat centres and door and rear side panels were upholstered in a special cloth, bordered by leather seat side sections and head-rests. Other interior parts were finished in silver, and standard equipment included front electric windows, central locking, power steering, an on-board computer, ABS anti-lock brakes and stove enamelled centres to the cross-spoked alloy wheels. Under the bonnet a three-way catalytic converter was fitted as standard equipment for the first time on the UK market. (All subsequent M3s delivered to Britain would hereafter feature this refinement to their specification, requiring the exclusive use of unleaded fuel.)

The next turning point in the development of the M3 came in early 1990 when a run of 600 M3 Sport Evolutions were produced, fitted with a 95 × 87mm, 2,467cc engine developing 238bhp at 7,000rpm in road trim. This latest homologation special not only enabled the M3 to take maximum advantage of the 2.5-litre capacity maximum prevailing in the German and Italian national saloon car championships, but it also enabled BMW to homologate adjustable spoilers front and rear for racing purposes.

Additional body stiffening assures the M3 coupe's strucural rigidity on a par with the saloon.

There is still adequate room for two adults in the rear passenger compartment despite the packaging for the hood mechanism.

For the 1991 season, the M3's 2.5-litre engine had its output raised yet again to the point that it was producing 360bhp at 9,500rpm in German Touring Car Championship Group A guise. Its maximum torque remained unchanged at 214lb/ft but the maximum engine speed was increased slightly to a 9,500rpm limit. The ECU engine management system developed by BMW Motorsport GmbH also incorporated an enlarged memory for the new season as well as a dry-sump lubrication system.

In the interests of enhanced weight distribution, the fuel tank was moved to a new position at the rear of the car, where it is divided into two sections, the larger of which is fitted in the same place as the standard tank.

Using Finite element analysis, the roll cage incorporated within the M3 racer comprises some 82ft (25m) of stable tubes. This effectively offers the driver the additional protection and security of an inner, secondary spaceframe, to which all the key suspension components are attached.

The fielding of these latest specification M3s was entrusted to two works teams, one semi-works team and continued support for private teams in the form of a supply of BMW contracted works drivers. BMW M Team Schnitzer would field Johnny Cecotto, Joachim Winkelhock and Kris Nissen. The Italian-based BMW M Team Bigazzi would field Britain's Steve Soper and Armin Hahne, while the Linder M Team used Altfrid Heger, the veteran Dieter Quester, and the most consistent lady driver so far entered for the German Championship, Annette Meeuvissen. Support was also given to the Isert team, fielding Prince Leopold of Bavaria, and the MM Diebels Team, who had BMW works drivers Christian Danner and Otto Rensing at their disposal with BMW Motorsport underwriting their driving fees for this programme.

ROUND UP

The 1990 season had seen Johnny Cecotto finish runner-up in the German Championship – a contest governed by quite complicated regulations, whereby weight penalties are imposed on cars that prove consistently successful in an attempt to keep the competition well balanced. In 1991 the best-placed M3 driver in the German Championship turned out to be Steve Soper, in third place behind Audi's Frank Biela and Mercedes driver Klaus Ludwig. In the prestigious manufacturers' contest, BMW wound up second, this time to Mercedes who had a consistently successful season with their 190E 2.5-litre machines, but ahead of Audi.

In Britain, of course, the M3 emerged victorious in the national touring car championship thanks to the efforts of Will Hoy's Vic Lee Motorsport-entered example. The British series was being run to a 2-litre maximum, the M3 engine conforming to these rules by means of a reduction in stroke, and developing around 270bhp at 8,500rpm in this configuration.

As the original square-cut M3 was contesting the 1991 international season, a race-modified 'new shape' 3-series BMW racing prototype was undergoing intensive evaluation tests at Monza in the hands of multiple Touring Car Champion Roberto Ravaglia. These were intended to determine a specification to be homologated for the next generation M3. The speculation was that the car would be run in the German Championship as early as 1992.

However, sources close to BMW Motorsport suggest that the second generation M3 will not appear until the second half of 1992, to be homologated for 1993 with a 2.9-litre six-cylinder engine intended to sustain the competitive force of BMW's distinctive M-series identification well into the final decade of the century.

8   The M3 to the Test

When the first BMW M3s trickled on to the British market in the early months of 1987, Motorsport's homologation special seemed, on the face of it, an expensive indulgence at £22,750 tax paid. It was admittedly a couple of thousand pounds less expensive than the Mercedes-Benz 190E 2.3-16, the Porsche 944S and even the much-admired Renault GTA V6 Turbo, but its closest competitor had to be regarded as the Ford Sierra RS Cosworth.

At £17,100 on the road, this fastest Sierra derivative had burst on to the scene a year earlier to universal acclaim, combining shattering performance and leech-like road manners at what seemed a bargain basement price. Nevertheless, as *Autocar*'s testers concluded, the BMW M3 was judged to represent a remarkable combination of performance, refinement and practicality. Its price tag might seem high, they opined, but it was certainly a lot of motor car for the money. The comprehensive and penetrating text of their assessment was as follows.

ROAD TEST
Autocar
15 April 1987

The launch of the BMW M3 marks an historic moment for the Bavarian manufacturer, since this is the first BMW to be developed by the motor sports division and produced by BMW AG.

The M3 is seen as a successor to the legendary M1 – a competition inspired machine – but the M3 is much more a production racer. BMW has made every attempt to make the car

as civilized as possible for everyday driving. It may have the latest innovations in its make-up to ensure highly competitive track performance, but BMW has deliberately not compromised comfort or equipment levels.

The 2.3-litre, 16-valve engine, developing no fewer than 200bhp at 6,750rpm, easily puts the M3 at the top of the 3-series performance league.

The general exterior specification, which includes distinctive wheel arch flares (designed to accommodate up to 10in wheels in full race trim), extended sills, front and rear air dams, plus light alloy wheels and low profile tyres, ensures a further degree of exclusivity. In addition, BMW has carefully raked the rear screen to give a coupe appearance to the two-door shell. The boot is now slightly shorter and the lid higher.

Under the steel shell and composite body add-ons, BMW has paid particular attention to good directional stability. Wheel castor is increased three-fold, the anti-roll bars are a larger diameter and the steering modified to give increased feel.

Apart from the tuned shock absorbers and rear springs, the rear axle assembly is the same as other 3-series BMWs. The brake system, however, is not. Both front and rear discs are bigger and thicker, with reinforced calipers. Larger 5-series-size wheel bearings are incorporated on special front stub axles for increased durability.

Inside, equipment levels are high with central locking, electric windows, door mirrors and slide and tilt steel sunroof as standard. There's also a leather-rimmed steering wheel and gearknob, hide-trimmed seats front and rear, plus a Blaupunkt radio/cassette player with four speakers and electric aerial.

Standard safety items include ABS anti-lock brakes and a limited slip differential, designed to operate with 25 per cent locking action.

BMW does not offer any extras with the M3 (although metallic paint is a no-cost option). The high standard spec goes some way to justifying the £22,750 price tag, £5,000 more than the next most expensive model in the 3-series, the 325iX four door.

Performance

With 200bhp to play with in a car weighing under 25cwt, performance is naturally one of the M3's strong suits. Our mean maximum speed of 139mph was achieved in driving rain on a very wet track, and there would certainly be another couple of mph to come in ideal conditions – BMW in fact claims 146mph. At the best one-way speed of 140mph, the engine is spinning at 6,600rpm, just 150rpm below the power peak which demonstrates near-ideal gearing.

The Bosch Motronic management system incorporates a rev limiter set at an indicated 7,300rpm, coinciding with the start of the solid red sector, although the broken line starts at 7,000rpm. We took 7,000rpm as the limit for our in-gears figures, and this equates to maximum speeds of 40, 62, 84 and 118mph.

Standing starts were conducted on a still-damp track and yielded a mean 0–60mph time of 7.1secs. 0–30mph still came up in 2.8secs though, with perhaps only another 0.3secs to come off that on a perfectly dry surface. This compares well with BMW's quoted 6.7secs to 62mph and shows the superior traction of rear-wheel drive in the wet – a powerful front-wheel-drive car would have been lucky to get within a second of its potential in such conditions.

The close-ratio Getrag five-speed gearbox has a dog-leg first, and the gearchange is sprung to the centre 2nd/3rd gear plane. The gate is rather vague and it was all too easy to

find fourth instead of second when going for a quick ratio swap. Obviously the box was designed with competition use in mind, where first is used only on the starting grid, but for normal road use it does require some care.

The M3's 200bhp from a 2.3-litre normally aspirated engine might seem like a recipe for a very peaky power delivery, but this is far from the case. The 16-valve unit is in fact extremely flexible, and will pull without hesitation from well below 1,000rpm.

Its mid-range punch is very impressive indeed, as a glance at the in-gear acceleration figures will confirm, and the power is, of course, delivered without any troublesome turbo-lag. In third gear for example, the M3 will accelerate from 50–70mph in 4.1secs, and in top gear each 20mph increment from 20–90mph takes less than 10 secs.

Economy

For a car offering this sort of performance, an overall fuel consumption figure of over 20mpg is very good indeed. Our figure of 20.3mpg includes the speed-testing sessions and is a tribute to the efficiency of the 16-valve engine and its Bosch management system. The average owner could certainly expect over 22mpg, giving a range of 300 miles from the 15.4 gallon tank.

Refinement

Given that the M3 is an homologation car, on sale to ensure the BMW's inclusion in Group A saloon car racing, you might expect it to have a few rough edges. But as 5,000 examples have to be produced, BMW obviously needed to make the M3 an acceptable road car to avoid a huge financial loss on the project. As a result, the car has been built to provide the standards of luxury that a BMW owner expects, and that includes the levels of refinement.

The engine, although it can't match the

*The M3 Sport Evolution heralded
the arrival of the 2.5-litre four-cylinder
engine at the start of 1990.*

(Opposite) *M3 Sport Evolution was expressly
designed for homologation of the more
powerful engine and added aerodynamic
downforce for competition purposes.*

occupying the spot normally filled by the economy gauge in lesser BMWs. In all other respects, the instrument layout is similar to most other 3-series cars.

That includes column stalks either side of the wheel. The right-hand item handles wash/wipe if pulled, single flick wipe if pushed down, plus intermittent and two-speed wiper settings if lifted up. The left stalk takes care of indicators and dip/main beam settings with the actual lights switch sited in the dash at the extreme left.

The driving position feels just right; the wheel position is sensible and there is enough seat adjustment to cater for most sizes. The pedals are well placed for heel-and-toe changes and when the clutch is dormant, there is a large foot-rest to the left of the pedal. Headroom is adequate for drivers up to 6ft in height, but not for those taller than this. You can tilt the seat slightly to gain more clearance, but at the expense of spoiling the driving position.

Ergonomically speaking, there is not much wrong with the M3's layout – all the major controls are within easy reach, the door pulls are conveniently angled so a user does not have to strain to close the door, and the interior handles are flush fitting with no nasty sharp edges to rub against.

Convenience

Arguably, this is the only area where the M3 falls down, with its boot space restricted by the more raked rear window, which also leads to a smaller load aperture with the bootlid raised. Like other 3-series BMW models the M3 does not have much in the way of rear passenger space. Headroom is at a premium and with the front seats well back on their runners there is virtually no legroom despite the fact that the front seat back-rests are cut out to help.

The rear seats are individually shaped and the M3 is clearly intended as no more than a four-seater at most.

In other respects convenience levels match those of the standard 3-series models and includes adequate cubby space with reasonably sized door pockets, glove box and the odd moulded tray in the centre console. The heating and ventilation controls include turn wheels for the four-speed fan and temperature adjustment, with three additional sliders for direction.

On the most powerful setting, the fan delivers a very impressive blast for quick demisting or rapid changes in temperature. On the first two settings it also works unobtrusively enough not to detract from overall refinement levels. The standard equipment electric windows take just four seconds to raise via the push buttons mounted conveniently on the centre console. The roof mounted controls for the powered sunroof are a little more awkward to find and require a driver to look up from the road to operate. The small controls for the powered door mirrors are more conveniently placed atop the driver's door pull. Mirrors, washer nozzles and the driver's door lock are all heated to prevent icing up in wintry conditions.

Under the boot lid there is adequate space for two medium-sized suitcases, but available space is hindered by the inclusion of boxes on either side, one for the battery, the other for the jack. The spare wheel is hidden under the carpeted load compartment floor.

The forward hinging bonnet lifts to reveal the very impressive sight of the powerful 2.3-litre four and routine servicing looks straightforward enough, although the air box needs to be removed to get at the oil filter. Spark plug removal is far easier and the oil dipstick and fluid levels in the various reservoirs are easily checked.

Safety

Besides aiding the aerodynamic qualities and reducing the drag coefficient to cd 0.3, the wraparound body add-ons are also designed with safety in mind. The three-piece

A thicker-rimmed steering wheel is the distinctive feature of the M3 Sport Evolution cabin.

M-Sport striping extends even to gearchange knob!

The muted twin-nostril nose treatment continues the established BMW theme.

The M3's forged alloy cross-spoked road wheel.

M3 Sport Evolution rear spoiler with raised tail section in place.

Traditional M-Series badging on the boot lid.

front bumper is a composite structure comprising an energy-absorbing foam impact block and a skin of glass-fibre reinforced polyurethane foam. The rear bumper, integrated into the undervalance, is made in the same way and of similar materials. Thanks to this design just one single bumper is required to fulfil all legal standards and regulations worldwide, including the very strict US standards.

The light alloy wheels feature hidden studs behind the removable wheel centre and thereby adding a degree of security against theft.

Verdict

Stepping into the BMW M3 is a bit like pulling on a well-fitting glove, one of those rare occurrences when a driver instantly feels at home behind the wheel. The driving position is right and when you begin to use the power and experience the handling you begin to feel part of the car.

The M3 is perhaps the most successful

homologation-inspired road/racer offered by a manufacturer to date. The car is as docile in town as any driver could wish and easy to manoeuvre due to its compact proportions. Then when you hit the open road and pour on the power, the chassis handles all the demands a driver makes upon it, whatever the road surface. In this respect BMW has arrived at an excellent compromise in suspension settings, bearing in mind the car's raison d'etre.

The fact of the matter is that the M3 makes a very sensible road car; it looks the part with its decidedly sporty styling, it is not over the top and very purposeful.

In road trim the M3 may not have the legs of the Sierra Cosworth but what it lacks in performance it more than compensates for with its easier road manners and better directional stability at speed. The Mercedes 190E 2.3-16 can match the BMW in this respect but its engine of similar specification is less responsive thanks to the larger and heavier body. Nor is the Mercedes as nimble as the BMW.

9 The M3 Goes Rallying

When the first M3s came off the production line in early 1986, BMW had no thoughts at all about a rallying application for the car. Wolfgang Peter Flohr was at that time Managing Director of BMW Motorsport and nothing could have been further from his mind, although a French-developed M1 had been used on several French tarmac rallies, and even competed in the Tour de Corse, back in 1982, in the hands of Bernard Darniche.

'BMWs were not perceived as cars that flew half a metre in the air, carrying twenty-five foglights and covered in dirt,' he explained with a grin. 'We were not interested in rallying at all; that was the preserve of the Group B cars and such four-wheel-drive cars as BMW possessed were designed for road rather than competition use.' Rallying had not been in their marketing philosophy.

However, FISA President Jean-Marie Balestre decreed that the spectacular Group B supercars would be outlawed in the aftermath of the tragic accident which claimed the life of Henri Toivonen and his co-driver, when their Lancia crashed on the Tour de Corse rally. It was the general view that these machines, whilst spectacular and appealing to the spectator, were just too quick. International rallying would be toned down with the introduction of Group A regulations for the 1987 season and, suddenly, the M3 looked as though it might have a competitive application, away from the world of touring car racing.

BACK ON THE TRACKS

It was the British Prodrive organization, headed by experienced rallyist Dave Richards from premises in Banbury, that first approached BMW with the idea of using the M3 in a rallying application, with the French Championship in mind. With a proliferation of tarmac events, it quickly became clear that four-wheel drive wasn't always a necessary prerequisite for success.

As a result of this imaginative approach, Prodrive was able to give BMW its first World Championship Rally victory when Bernard Beguin emerged victorious. Cynics would say that the Tour de Corse, like so many European rallies, is more akin to a controlled road race, so perhaps it is not surprising that the M3's agile handling properties should prove a decisive factor.

Prodrive's rallying M3s were initially developed by Chief Engineer David Lapworth to deliver 285bhp at 8,400rpm on a 12:1 compression ratio, driving through a six-speed purpose-built gearbox and a carbon multi-plate clutch and a Prodrive-developed limited slip differential. At 2,260lb (1,025kg) the cars compared very favourably in terms of weight with the competing Audi 200 Quattro, the Sierra Cosworth RS and the Lancia Delta HF Integrale.

Unquestionably, the BMW M3's greatest rallying achievement was its victory at the 1987 Tour de Corse. The achievement was described in detail within the pages of the respected *Rallycourse* annual:

The M3's great rallying moment! Bernard Beguin's Prodrive-prepared machine
en route *to a memorable victory on the 1987 Tour de Corse.*

Theoretically, a powerful rear-wheel-drive car should always be a potential winner in Group A on tarmac. Yet few teams have successfully developed such machinery, and none but David Richards's Prodrive operation has gone further still and won a World Championship event. Nevertheless, it would be a trifle misleading to describe Bernard Beguin's convincing win in Corsica as a rare victory for a privateer. Certainly his BMW M3 wasn't entered by the factory, but while the transforming of the M3 from racing car to rally car was largely to Richards's credit, he was fully supported by BMW, engines and other major components being supplied from Munich.

That isn't intended to belittle winning in Corsica. Prodrive might be well drilled and well financed, but it remains one of the few non-works teams one can compare to the major factories. The rally BMW began testing barely two months before Corsica, making it the newest car with a chance of victory on the event, although the fortunes of some of its rivals might have suggested otherwise.

Although only setting fastest time on nine of the event's twenty-four special stages, Beguin's M3 won by 2min 8sec, heading home a couple of Lancia Delta HF Turbos. The following year Beguin would be back in

BMW's link with the Brabham Formula 1 team enabled them to use Brabham's facilities to crash test an F1 chassis for the first time. The lessons learned in destroying this Brabham BT49 were incorporated in the design of the BMW-engined BT52, which won the Championship for the Munich company in 1983.

Neerpasch at BMW. The Formula 1 project couldn't be revived in the short term, even though Lauda went on German television with what amounted to a thinly veiled plea for the Board to think again.

BOMBSHELL

In 1979, Neerpasch made the decision to move on to take a similar post with the French Talbot company. Neerpasch recommended to BMW Sales Director Hans-Erdmann Schoenbeck that Dieter Stappert, his number two, should take his place when he departed. But then Neerpasch dropped a bombshell. Talbot was proposing to acquire the rights to the BMW 1.5-litre turbo project. Stappert remonstrated against this vociferously and embarked on a highly successful campaign to get the deal stamped on, a task in which he proved tremendously successful. Mercifully for Stappert's ambitions, the agreement had not progressed to the stage of a formal contract.

On 24 April 1980, BMW announced that it would be building and supplying engines for Formula 1. The man charged with the development of the 1.5-litre turbo concept was Paul Rosche, who had become General Manager of BMW Motorsport at the instigation of Neerpasch back in 1975.

Dieter Stappert

This gentle, bespectacled and highly respected former journalist presided successfully over BMW's great days as Formula 1 engine suppliers in the early 1980s.

Stappert made his name as editor of the respected Swiss motorsporting magazine *Powerslide*. Yet by 1977 he knew he had exhausted his journalistic potential. He first received an offer to join BMW back in 1975, but he decided to stick it out in journalism.

While he was ill in hospital in 1977, Neerpasch got in touch and asked him whether he would be interested in joining BMW as his assistant. This time Dieter had no hesitation in accepting. He joined BMW Motorsport on 13 July 1977.

Stappert's initial responsibilities involved working with the BMW Junior team. Through much of 1979 Stappert was heavily involved in the M1 Procar series, which supported several of the European Formula 1 Grands Prix. But, away from the rough and tumble of this particular programme, other developments were simmering away behind the scenes.

The debacle over the Lauda/McLaren proposal in 1979, followed by Neerpasch's departure, left the job open for Stappert. So Stappert took over as head of the Formula 1 programme.

It was a position he accepted with alacrity, although he had to fight tooth and nail to prevent the Formula 1 project from going with Neerpasch to his new employers. As things turned out, Dieter's long battle to keep the engine paid off when, in April 1980, the BMW board confirmed that the company would be building and supplying engines to Formula 1.

The decision was taken to form an alliance with the British Brabham team owned by Bernie Ecclestone, President of the FOCA. Nevertheless, Stappert had to contend with unpredictable political forces within Formula 1, at a time when the teams were being dragged reluctantly into the turbo era. The gestation period for the BMW four-cylinder turbo engine proved to be uncomfortably protracted and fraught with mechanical failures.

Fortunately, Stappert had a great deal of confidence in Piquet's singlemindedness and commitment. The first Brabham-BMWs raced in the 1982 South African Grand Prix. The season saw the team initially dart back and forth between using these new machines and its older, proven, Cosworth V8-engined cars.

Later that season there were more problems. Piquet had failed to qualify for the Detroit Grand Prix and Gordon Murray showed some reluctance to run the BMW-engined car in the following weekend's Canadian Grand Prix. Thankfully, the BMW turbo engine, it turned out, did win that particular race.

There had been times over the previous year when divorce had seemed to be staring Brabham and BMW in the face, when Stappert had looked like the meat in an uncompromising sandwich with a sometimes cynical and sarcastic Ecclestone and a bemused BMW board providing the bread which squeezed him hard from both directions.

Now the partnership was up and running and, in 1983, Nelson Piquet would drive a Brabham-BMW to the first turbo World Championship. Stappert gained a great deal of satisfaction at being involved in such a momentous achievement, but the job was proving an enormous strain for him and he eventually decided to leave BMW in 1985 to pursue other interests. In any case, by this time the Brabham team's decision to switch to Pirelli tyres significantly undermined their competitiveness, and BMW scored only a single F1 victory in 1985 when Piquet won the French Grand Prix at Paul Ricard.

Dieter Stappert's calm and unflustered approach to the political side of BMW's Formula 1 involvement enabled the programme to run a lot more smoothly than it otherwise would. These days, the genial Swiss is back on his original side of the motor racing fence, as a journalist and television commentator!

Of course, BMW's determination to link their high-performance image to road car technology virtually guaranteed that there was never any chance of a BMW Grand Prix engine being anything but derived from a road power unit. The manufacture of an esoteric, purpose-built, multi-cylinder engine might well have offered scope for more long-term success, but as BMW's advertising campaigns had already emphasized throughout their Formula 1 involvement, the link between the four-cylinder production engine and the racing programme was of crucial significance.

BMW had first become seriously involved in Formula 2 in 1973, when Jean-Pierre Jarier won the European Championship in a works March fitted with a 2-litre production block-derived engine. BMW would continue to provide the Championship engines in this category in 1974 (Patrick Depailler), 1975 (Jacques Laffite), 1978 (Bruno Giacomelli), 1979 (Marc Surer) and 1982 (Corrado Fabi).

By the end of this period, the works March-BMW Formula 2 cars were firmly identified with the M-Sport theme. The cars sported the 'BMW MPower' logo on their cam covers and air boxes plus 'MPower, MStyle, MDesign and MTechnic' livery on the bodywork. The link between this racing progamme and the BMW 3-series saloons was put into splendid focus by a contemporary BMW advertisement and titled 'Now there's more than one way into a BMW Sports car'.

THE BMW M12/13

Using McLaren Engines' development data, in addition to the information BMW had accumulated through building turbocharged touring car engines in Europe, Rosche confidently took his first steps forward with the four-cylinder BMW M12/13 project – this designation identifying it as the thirteenth version of the original M12 engine design.

It took only a short time for the BMW Motorsport engineers to discover that these standard production blocks performed best when they were two or three years old, perhaps with as much as 60,000 miles (100,000km) under their belt in road use. It seemed that the mileage and ageing helped remove the inherent tensions and stresses within the block material. Therefore, an artificial 'ageing' process was evolved and, apart from removing around 11lb (5kg) of superfluous metal, such as stiffening ribs and water channels on the inlet side, these new Formula 1 engines were based on unmodified road car blocks.

The twin overhead camshaft, four-valves per cylinder unit had a bore and stroke of 89.2×60mm, officially rated at 1,499cc. It incorporated a steel crankshaft running in five main bearings with short, forged alloy Mahle pistons and very rugged titanium connecting rods. With a compression ratio of 6.7:1, the BMW M12/13 initially developed 557bhp at 9,500rpm using a single turbocharger, manufactured by Kuhlne, Kopp and Kausch, positioned low on the left-hand side of the engine.

The injection system employed a Bosch electric high-pressure pump for starting up and a Lucas mechanical pump then took over, driven directly from the inlet camshaft. An agreement was reached to supply the works Brabham team with these engines. Nelson Piquet tested the first Brabham-BMW prototype during practice for the 1981 British Grand Prix at Silverstone, but it would not be until the following season's South African Grand Prix at Kyalami that the combination made its Formula 1 racing debut.

TURBO YEARS

The BMW M12/13 engine had arrived on the Grand Prix scene during a transitional phase in which it was difficult for teams to judge whether it was better to hang on using a light, nimble or naturally aspirated car, or throw all their resources into the turbo development

BMW Motorsport's M12/13 Formula 1 four-cylinder turbo made its debut at the 1982 South African Grand Prix at Kyalami, installed in the Brabham BT50 chassis.

programme. Clearly, the turbo promised a long-term assurance of success, but the Brabham-BMW partnership was subject to this rocky uncertainty during the course of the 1982 season, as the team switched back and forth between the turbo and their old Cosworth V8-engined car.

Eventually, the partnership very nearly came apart at the seams when Piquet failed to qualify the Brabham-BMW for the inaugural Detroit Grand Prix. However, the following weekend he took the car to victory in the Canadian Grand Prix at Montreal, setting the scene for a partnership which would last through to the end of 1987.

In 1983 Nelson became the first driver to win the World Championship at the wheel of a turbocharged car, his Brabham-BMW BT52. The last Grand Prix to be won by a BMW engine was the 1986 Mexican race when Gerhard Berger emerged victorious at the wheel of his Benetton B186. By now,

sky-high turbo boost pressure had raised the output of the tiny production-based BMW four-cylinder engine to well in excess of 1,000bhp for short bursts during qualifying – a quite remarkable testament to the fundamental soundness of the basic cylinder block on which the project had originally been based.

For the 1986 season Gordon Murray had designed his 'lowline' Brabham BT55 for which BMW Motorsport had produced a specially adapted M12/13/1 four-cylinder engine laying over at an angle of 72 degrees. Unfortunately, pre-season testing was grossly disrupted by problems with the new bevel-drive transmission and, while the car's smaller frontal area should have helped matters, the canted BMW engine suffered from serious oil scavenge problems which absorbed an excessive amount of power. Development never really caught up over the course of the season and, while

Index